P9-CRO-738

Reference Check 2.0

How Digital Social Networking is Transforming the Selection Process

By Yves Lermusi

Copyright © 2009 by Checkster. Printed in the United States of America. Except as permitted under the United States Copyright Act of 1976, no part of this publication may be reproduced or distributed in any form or by any means, or stored in a data base or retrieval system, without the prior written permission of the publisher.

Table of Contents

Objective:

Demonstrate how the
Reference Check 2.0
process improves
Talent Management

"When interviewing people for a job position in your company, it is critical to know about their past jobs. Remember, the best predictor of current behavior is past behavior. You want to know what they excelled at, what, if anything, went wrong, and what other people thought of them. Many people have blinders to their own weaknesses, so talking with others can provide essential information. Reference checks are a key component of good business."

—*neuroscientist Daniel Amen*

"We did a regression test on what was the best predictor of performance with the interview score, the references, their background,… and we basically found that their background and references are the best predictors…"

Marissa Mayer, V.P. of Search Product
and User Experience at Google

Introduction

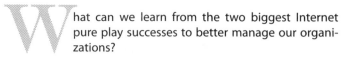hat can we learn from the two biggest Internet pure play successes to better manage our organizations?

Search and digital social networks are at the center of the Internet. What can we learn from them in order to run our organizations better and only hire top performers?

This book will show you what you can learn from these two core applications in order to transform your selection process and reach the highest hiring and internal promotion success you ever had.

What made Google overtake Yahoo for online search at a time when Yahoo was celebrated as the clear winner? Is there a lesson you can learn from the Google algorithm that could transform your business accordingly?

We will start this journey by understanding the Google algorithm and how you can benefit from it. At the center of this new paradigm is the concept of collective intelligence.

How can we leverage digital social networks to run better organizations?

Today, many individuals are more likely to have the email address of a colleague than a phone number. In addition, they are more likely to ask questions or keep them updated through an asynchronous online mechanism than through real time face-to-face meetings or phone conversations. How can we leverage this shift to keep our processes efficient and effective?

We will see that the digital social networks are the new enablers of collective intelligence gathering.

These two new powerful practices will help us understand how we can expand the Reference Check 1.0 process or the previous process of staged reference calls to a truly collective intelligence exercise. Understanding the limitation of the Reference Check 1.0 will lead us to uncover the power of the Reference Check 2.0 and its new possibilities.

At the essence of this short book lie three principles by which to transform your reference check practice into something that really works so that your organization can become a Reference Check 2.0 organization:

1. **Ask the right questions** or focus on **_what to ask_**. A sample questionnaire is given in Appendix 1. In short, focus on performance and not skills or knowledge.

2. **Leverage new technologies** and digital social network intelligence to automate the reference check process or enable new tools to support **_how to ask_** those questions. A process example and report are in Appendix 4 and 5.

3. **Perform the check** at the right time in your process. As a consequence of the automation gained from the previous point, you are not penalized for running more checks. Run the checks when you can still act on them, or **on the finalists**, or make sure your timing is right on **_when to ask_** to perform a checkup. Section 11.1 shows that 15 percent of organizations already took this leap forward.

So **to summarize,** the Google algorithm shows that collective intelligence really works, while social networks prove that the digital medium adds an efficient method for social interaction. These two processes lead to a rebirth of the reference check into what we call Reference Check 2.0.

One-sentence summary: **Reference Check 2.0 is a natural extension of Internet evolution.**

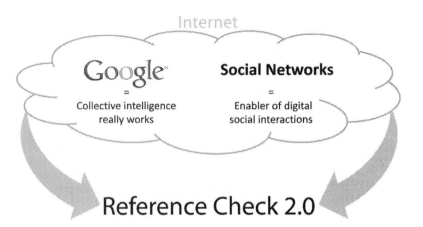

Fig 1. Two main Internet successes naturally lead to the Reference Check 2.0 process

1 Google's Algorithm in one page

Google was able to become the online default search destination for two main reasons: its usability and algorithm.

To explain its algorithm, simply start with a target: the search terms. The search terms represent the goal, the target of what you're after.

Once you define the target, the results that the algorithm gives you are computed according to the amount of endorsements a certain site receives. The more endorsement a site receives, the higher it will appear on the list of search results. The endorsements are simply measured by the weighted number of hyperlinks leading to that page. In other words, the endorsements or recommendations here are understood as a link that represents the essence of the Google algorithm. The results will show as a list of ranked pages, the most valuable one on top. Let's see how Google describes it:

> PageRank relies on the uniquely democratic nature of the web by using its vast link structure as an indicator of an individual page's value. In essence, Google interprets a link from page A to page B as a vote, by page A, for page B. But, Google looks at more than the sheer volume of votes, or links a page receives; it also analyzes the page that casts the vote. Votes cast by pages that are themselves "important" weigh more heavily and help to make other pages "important."[1]

The wisdom of the crowd as demonstrated in the statement above creates way more value than any human classification can, even that which is made by professionals. That is how Google was successful at outpacing Yahoo in the search business.

However, today we see Google's limits, as many advertisers are trying to game the system and are often successful at it. This is because collective intelligence must respect a couple of principles[2] to be efficient. Three key principles must be respected if one is to rely on a group of people to establish ranking: authenticity, diversity and discernment.

---

[1] http://en.wikipedia.org/wiki/PageRank
[2] http://www.community-intelligence.com/blogs/public/2004/05/notes_on_factors_in_collective.html#more

Each emoticon represents an independent page, and each arrow represents a hyperlink. The green page receives the most number of incoming links, so it has the highest page rank. The yellow has the second highest number of incoming links, so it ranks at #2. The red one has the least number of incoming links, so it ranks the lowest.

Fig 2. The Google algorithm in one image

Authenticity: this is understood as the ability of each participant to be free to express his or her real thoughts, and to not be engaged in a hidden agenda or deceptive tactics.

Diversity: not simply in terms of gender or ethnic background, but also when it comes to diversity of knowledge, experience, personality, cognitive style, etc.

Discernment: even if you assemble a diverse group that can be authentic, the results will be enhanced if you can improve discernment. In other words, enable participants to discern difference and relevance. This is often achieved by using a framework.

So **to summarize**, the Google algorithm relies on an age-old and proven model: the democratic model. However, in order for it to work, you have to respect a couple of principles. The main ones are authenticity, diversity and discernment.

One-sentence summary: **there is wisdom in collective intelligence.**

2 Digital social Networks in one page

I f e-mail was truly the killer app of the Internet, social networks would be what gives it meaning.

According to Wikipedia, a social network is *"a social structure made of nodes (which are generally individuals or organizations) that are tied by one or more specific type of interdependency, such as values, visions, ideas, financial exchange, friendship, sexual relationships, kinship, dislike, conflict or trade."*

Social networks are often narrowly understood as networks of updated connections. But the mere benefits of having an up-to-date address book is far from the true power social networks can deliver. What social networks have demonstrated is the willingness of people to share, participate, provide feedback, and truly embrace meaningful communication about many subjects.

We will not discuss the role that social networks can have in building an identity and fulfilling powerful, basic individual needs[3]. Instead, we will look at applications that digital social networks enhance beyond simple personal needs in order to benefit a larger group of people.

One of the first and most well-known shared benefits of a social network (even if it was not promoted under the term social network) can be seen in the rating tool that eBay and Amazon provide its customers. They become interdependent on their shopping experience or transaction. Consequently, these ratings are truly impacting how people purchase and where they purchase from. Yet, these ratings are only possible as long as the nodes (buyers) are actively involved in the process. Netflix, Yelp, and many other recommendation systems are based on the same principle. In these cases, the interdependency results in a great movie or evening out, since buyers have already rated certain movies or places of interest.

In order for us to see how social networks can be leveraged within organizations, let's look at three marketplaces for contractors: ELance, Guru, and Odesk. Elance, Guru, and Odesk are online

---

[3] http://blogs.harvardbusiness.org/now-new-next/2009/03/the-ancient-psychological-root.html

Social networks in their digital format are a collective intelligence enabler.

Fig 3. Digital social Networks in one image

sites designed for contractors and employers to meet. Although the main focus is on realizing a contractual transaction, each site has a feedback tool that allows the interdependency of its users to be optimized, resulting in a successful contract.

Social media consequently provides a perfect venue in which the Google algorithm or the wisdom of the crowd can thrive. The refinement of the rating can increase and go further than a simple link to provide incredible value.

> **To summarize,** digital social networks provide a frictionless environment that enables the implementation of Google's algorithm, or the creation of collective intelligence on many topics.
>
> One-sentence summary: **Digital social networks are collective intelligence enablers.**

3 How can it be applied to organizations?

We believe that organizations can benefit greatly from the two aforementioned lessons. They can leverage an organization's social network (the employee population itself) in order to optimize its performance. This can be its organizational structure, product innovation, production improvement, or individual performance.

In addition, they can help an organization leverage the entire workforce to market new products, find new sales leads, or find top performers by using existing social networks such as Linkedin or Facebook.

We will focus on the fundamental component of any organization: its employees.

By doing so, we will demonstrate how these two new lessons can be applied to an organization's employees in order to optimize organizational performance. We will focus on one decision or process that must happen in any organization: employee selection.

The selection of new team members, which is often described as critical in order to create any organization of quality, will be the focus of the rest of this book.

We will see how employee selection can be dramatically impacted by these new approaches to social networking and provide assistance to organizations and individuals. Since these social digital networks have the individual as its core component, it is a democratic system that empowers the individual while at the same time boosts the organization.

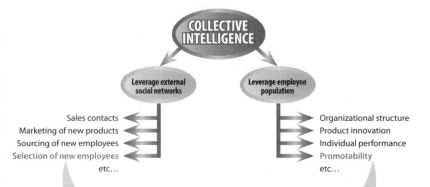

Collective intelligence can be leveraged through internal or external digital social networks. Many applications are possible, including the marketing of new products, the support of a sales process, and many other applications. This book will focus on the selection of new employees and the promotion of existing ones. These processes will rely on a process we call Reference Check 2.0.

Fig 4. Multiple usage of collective intelligence through social networks

> **To summarize,** we will focus on how applications that enhance collective intelligence through digital social networks assist organizations in the employee selection process.
>
> One-sentence summary: **Employee selection can benefit greatly from collective intelligence through digital social networks.**

4 Reference Check 2.0

Every organization today interviews their future employees. It is just inconceivable to bring someone in without having even spoken to them. However, we do know that about 50 percent of new hires are, on average, bad hires. Having acknowledged this fact, organizations have been implementing new processes in order to increase the success rate of new hires. Adding multiple rounds of structured interviews, assessments, work sample tests, virtual job tryouts or telephone reference checks are some of the things employers are doing to fully evaluate candidates. All of these are good, but they are also expensive and are often not justified by the extra expense and delay. That is why most organizations are not combining these methods and instead stick with the typical resume review and interview process. We will see in the following pages how the birth of the digital social network arms organizations with new possibilities to increase the accuracy of the selection process while only marginally increasing cost and time delay.

Referrals represent the number one source of new employees in organizations, and that has been the case for many years. This has been true even when we had all the digital means at our disposal. The main reason for this lies in the fact that a referral is not simply a piece of paper or words on a screen, for they intrinsically provide a quality description of the individual by one or several other individuals. That is why today you have about a 30 percent chance of getting hired if you are coming from a referral versus less than 1 percent if you are applying through the corporate website. This 30-to-1 ratio is a perfect example of the power people recommendation hold.

Unfortunately, in the world of employee selection, the recommendations of other people or previous colleagues, which are referred to as a reference check, have been seriously diminished by the fear of litigation; the difficulty to access people; and the perceived lack of authenticity.

Reference checking as a practice has been decreasing over the years and much skepticism surrounds its practice today. The main reason for this can be attributed to how it is performed, as it is often done at the tail end of the recruiting process as part of

	Outside Hire	Internal move or referrals
Success Rate	55-70%	80-90%
Primary Hiring Decision Criteria	Relevant Past Experience	Consistent Past Performance
	Personality & first impression	Respect earned over time with colleagues
Underlying Differences	Light on performance	Light on relevant experience
	Heavy on experience	Heavy on performance
Focus on	Having the Skills	Producing Results
Main Enablers	Resume & interview	Colleagues' peer rating

Adds authenticity & access to peers   Adds authenticity through confidentiality

Reference Check 2.0

Table Adapted from "Hire with your head", Lou Adler

Fig 5. Reference Check 2.0 add authenticity to existing processes

the background check, and is used more as an insurance policy than an assessment tool. Also, many people have been facing brick walls as many companies' policies prevent employees from participating in the reference check process, or providing an employer with meaningful feedback. This is a dreadful situation to be in, as it seriously diminishes the potential of any business. The U.S. marketplace is the most affected by this, especially because of its strong litigious environment. This situation is more serious than we want to admit to ourselves, as it cuts out one of the most powerful means for screening individuals. In our view it is also mainly because of the lack of authenticity many responses hold.

Fortunately, digital social networking is changing the way we conduct business, and we will show you in this book how to leverage this unique powerful business tool.

To summarize, peer rating rightly conducted is the most accurate way to assess employees. Fear of litigation and lack of authenticity has caused businesses to use it less and less over the years. Digital social networking is changing this.

One-sentence summary: **Employee peer rating is the best assessment method through digital social networks. We are calling it the Reference Check 2.0.**

5 Perception versus reality on selection effectiveness

The typical selection criteria that people believe are accurate in screening and recruiting new employees are in fact very different than what they are in reality.

Most people believe experience is the best predictor of performance, with over 95 percent of people mentioning experience as the #1 criterion to predict good performance. Although experience appears to be a very accurate and widely used way to screen new employees, it is actually one of the worst.

This leads us to ask ourselves why is it still so widely used?

We believe it is for two reasons. For one, many people confuse past experience with past performance. You may believe someone with 20 years of experience in a specific area will be better than someone with three years. Yet, research shows a weak correlation between performance and experience. Although experience is not irrelevant, it is certainly not the best way to assess new potential employees. The second reason it remains widely used today is due to the fact that it is the easiest and cheapest data to access. Indeed any resume will tell you in a couple of seconds where an individual has worked and what he or she has done. What resumes or bios however never give in a reliable fashion is the performance and achievement one attained during those years.

This is where a third party assessment of any individual can be of great value. Intuitively we know this, as we can easily select the couple of top performing colleagues if we have to create a new department for instance.

Research proves this as well, for "peer rating" is one of the best ways to assess people. We believe it is the best way because it combines performance with other intangibles like cultural fit or attitude.

If you combine it with other accurate methods such as structured interviews and work sample tests, then you have the best way to increase the odds of getting a great new hire.

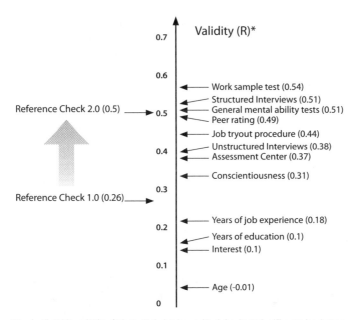

* Based on The Validity and Utility of Selection Methods in Personnel Psychology Practical and Theoretical Implications of 85 Years of Research Findings. Psychological Bulletin, Vol. 124, No. 2, 262-274

Fig 6. Accuracy of screening methods

To summarize, past work experience, education, or resumes are often seen as the most trusted sources of information in accurately selecting new team members. Yet, these are not the most accurate, but the easiest to access. Structured interviews, work sample tests, general mental abilities, and peer ratings are the most accurate.

One-sentence summary: **Structured interviews, work sample tests, general mental abilities and peer ratings are the best way to assess potential employees.**

6 Where accuracy meets efficiency

We've seen how work sample tests, structured interviews, general mental abilities and peer ratings achieve the highest level of selection accuracy. Yet, combining these four selection tools yields an even better level of accuracy. Unfortunately, in practice, using all four methods turns out to be too time consuming and overwhelming for managers, but luckily the digitalization of the social and work network has come to our rescue, enabling us to achieve a high level of accuracy while keeping time consumption low.

The method is simple yet very powerful. The ease of access that digital social networks enable provides the groundwork for performing solid and efficient peer rating. Obtaining information as is done in the peer rating process, is as easy as sending an email.

By placing emphasis on one's performance and not just experience, we come into a solid understanding of an individual, and thus provide a highly reliable way to assess people while marginally increasing effort.   And by doing this online — leveraging the digital social networks — it gives organizations a never before seen level of accuracy for the effort required.

The chart on the next page compares the time and cost associated with traditional assessment methods and the accuracy achieved. Everything above the horizontal dotted line has been proven to be accurate and has a correlation of 0.45 or more. Everything to the left of the vertical dotted line has a typical cost in time equivalent to 30 minutes or more per new talent identified.

Organizations strive for the best accuracy with the least cost output. This is outlined in the top right quadrant of the diagram, where the best process is in place. Yet, in order to keep the cost down, the process must be automated — that is where digital social network accessibility and some simple confidentiality treatment come into play.

Education and experience, featured in the bottom right quadrant of the diagram, are very quick and inexpensive methods, having

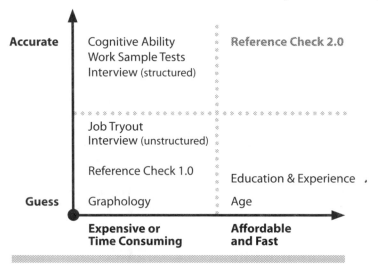

Fig 7. Accuracy & affordability of screening methods

a modest level of consistent accuracy are in the bottom right. Reference checking in its traditional form is expensive and limited in its accuracy — especially since most of the time current employers will not be included, yielding outdated information about the candidate.

Cognitive ability, work sample testing and structured job interviews are among the best predictors of a candidate's performance. Unfortunately, they are also either associated with the highest cost per new talent identified or are very time consuming. When translating these methods into salary equivalent or opportunity cost, the costs are far beyond what organizations are willing to spend at large.

> **To summarize:** Social networks, by the existing intelligence embedded in their structure and the fluidity of digital communication, enable a new way to gather highly accurate peer rating in an efficient way for new hire selection.
>
> One-sentence summary: **Peer rating that relies on social networks is the most accurate and efficient way to recognize talent. We call this the Reference Check 2.0.**

7 Comparison of Reference Check 1.0 and 2.0

The traditional process of reference checking involves four steps. First the recruiter or hiring manager will request references' information. Secondly, candidates will typically give the telephone numbers of three references. Then the recruiter or hiring manager will contact those references. Finally, they will compile a report. Contacting those references is by far the most difficult step in the process. Today, 97 percent of organizations do it by phone. Let's dissect in more detail each step of the reference checking process[4].

Reference Check 1.0	Reference Check 2.0
Asking for references & legal forms: Typically the request for references is performed either by phone or by e-mail. The requirements & forms are not automated. Employer time required: 11 min	**Asking for references & legal forms:** The future employer invites the individual to enter their references in an automated online tool via email. Requirements are automated. Employer time required: 2 min
Candidate provides the references: Each candidate goes in his or her address book and figures out who they will want to volunteer and see if they have the most updated information about these people. Employer time required: 0 min	**Candidate provides the references:** Each candidate goes in his or her address book or social network and imports up-to-date references. Employer time required: 0 min
The future employer calls the references: The series of calls and voicemails start before successfully reaching each other. Often a reference is ill prepared and pushed for time. Employer time required: 52 min (for 2.4 calls on average)	**Reference participates in an online confidential survey:** Each reference goes online at his or her convenience to take a confidential candid survey about the individual's performance. Employer time required: 0 min
Compile the report: Future employer often writes a report in an inconsistent fashion that documents their impression. They then forward it to the appropriate decision maker or file it. Employer time required: 14 min	**Compile the report:** The report is compiled automatically and provides a consistent approach. The Future employer can forward it to the appropriate decision maker or file it. Employer time required: 2 min

---

[4] Based on a survey performed by Checkster on 154 reference checking practitioners.

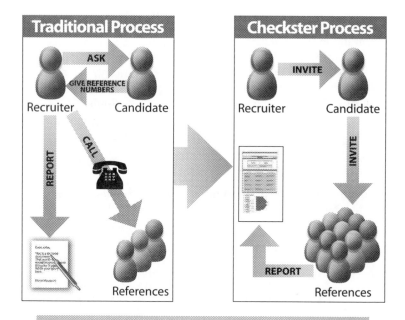

Fig 8. From a Reference Check 1.0 to a Reference Check 2.0 process

Digital social networks enable candidates to complement their e-mail address book with their social network connections. The benefits are mainly that the latest contact details are used and imported in bulk.

To summarize: Reference Check 1.0 is a less accurate and more time consuming method of performing a peer assessment today.

One-sentence summary: **Reference Check 2.0 saves organizations on average 73 minutes per reference check.**

8 Shortcomings of Reference Check 1.0

8.1 Getting in touch with the references:

Getting in touch with references is the most challenging part of performing a reference check the traditional way. As you can see on the chart, nobody sees it as very easy, and only 6 percent of people say that it is easy. On the other side, 65 percent of practitioners say that it is hard or very hard to perform.

According to our survey of 154 practitioners, it takes on average 20 minutes just to get in touch with the references. As many self reported time analysis surveys as there are, we believe that this is a conservative number.

To summarize: It is hard to get in touch with references in a timely fashion.

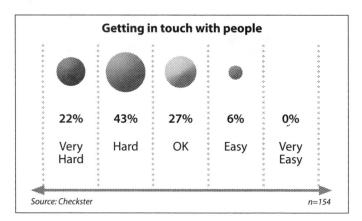

Getting in touch with people

22%	43%	27%	6%	0%
Very Hard	Hard	OK	Easy	Very Easy

Source: Checkster   n=154

8.2 Getting enough quality references:

Getting quality references is a big issue according to practitioners, as 61 percent say it is hard or very hard to perform. Thirty-one percent say it is okay while only 6 percent of people say that it is easy. With the traditional methods of reference checking, organizations request, on average, 3.2 references, as they try to reach three of them and only successfully connect with 2.4. The issue here is not only the number of references that is low but also the quality. Only requesting three references is also understandable because of the work it requires to reach each of them. Unfortunately, the combination of not obtaining enough references and the poor quality of references given jeopardizes the reliability of the output.

To summarize: It is hard to get enough quality references.

8.3 Getting enough useful information about the candidate:

Once you get in touch with the references, the next challenging part is to extract useful information. Again this is not easy for most practitioners, as 59 percent say that it is hard or very hard to perform. Only 7 percent of people say that it is easy or very easy. The fact that it is not confidential, people don't know each other, and of course some legal fears are involved, explain why most people find that this is not easy.

According to our survey of 154 practitioners, it takes on average 13 minutes to speak with the references.

To summarize: Even when references are contacted, the usefulness of the information is often marginal.

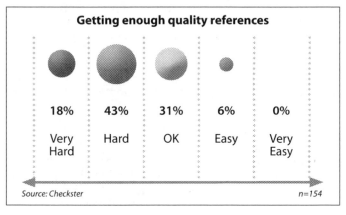

Getting enough quality references

18%	43%	31%	6%	0%
Very Hard	Hard	OK	Easy	Very Easy

Source: Checkster   n=154

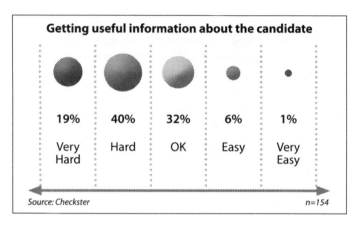

Getting useful information about the candidate

19%	40%	32%	6%	1%
Very Hard	Hard	OK	Easy	Very Easy

Source: Checkster   n=154

8.4 Report writing:

Report writing is mainly seen as an easy task, with 40 percent of practitioners describing it as easy or very easy to perform, and only 10 percent saying it is hard or very hard. The challenge here is more on the wasted time it represents and on the interpretation that can happen. Indeed each report requires about 14 minutes of the practitioner's time just for writing it. Another 11 minutes are also required to handle legal forms.

The value added of a practitioner writing reports is often minimal. If we also take into consideration the time required to handle legal forms, we have close to half an hour spent on purely administrative and low value added tasks. Consequently, we can say that while easy to perform, it is mainly a time waster especially when it can be automated.

To summarize: While easy to do, writing reports is a time waster.

8.5 Slow turnaround:

Not only is getting in touch with references time consuming, it also delays the whole process. Often, the telephone tag process will put the calls out for a couple of days. You may be lucky for a couple of them but on average the turnaround time is twice as long for the Reference Check 1.0 compared to the Reference Check 2.0. Indeed, the averge turnaround for the Reference Check 1.0 is four days, five hours, compared to two days, two hours for the Reference Check 2.0.

To summarize: Reference Check 1.0 turnaround time is twice as long as Reference Check 2.0.

One-sentence summary: **Reference Check 1.0 is hard to perform, takes a huge amount of time and provides only average quality outcome.**

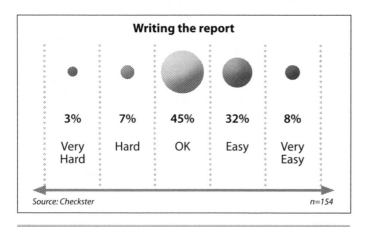

Source: Checkster   n=154

Fig 9. Shortcomings of Reference Check 1.0

9 When being good is a liability

Twenty-nine percent of practitioners like or even love to call people and perform Reference Check 1.0.

These 29 percent are often the best at it and will vocally oppose any change in a process they see as crucial. This creates tension within an organization, and we will see how this strength can become a liability if not overcome.

For the rest of the practitioners, performing reference checks is seen as a task that needs to be done and not faced with much enthusiasm.

As you can see on the chart, the majority of people see it as a pretty dull task (72 percent). Thirty percent don't like it at all and only 42 percent are okay with it. In short, performing reference checks is liked by 30 percent, hated by another 30 percent, and are seen as okay for the rest of practitioners.

That spread often makes the terrain for an interesting battle. Best performing practitioners who like the Reference Check 1.0 will oppose any change. A majority has no opinion. A minority hates it, but does not see the payback as big enough to fight the one liking it, as they often just don't do it, giving the traditional excuse of lack of time or not being able to reach the references.

This often puts the department in a position of liability for the organization.

It is a little bit like a door to door salesman resisting telesales, telling that the ratio of sales made is higher, but the number reached is so much lower that the best door to door sales man is doomed to become a poor performer. Paradoxically here, the best people at what they do (i.e. reference checking 1.0), when acting as a brake for a technology improvement and leveraging digital social networks with good intentions, will cripple their organization and their own future success.

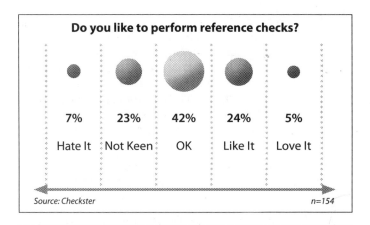

Fig 10. Do you like to perform Reference Check 1.0

To summarize: Performing Reference Check 1.0 is divided in the liking. Paradoxically, the best at it are likely to resist the evolution towards the Reference Check 2.0. This is when a strength can turn into a liability and leave the organization without a competitive process.

One-sentence summary: **1/3 of practitioners like to perform Reference Check 1.0 and will resist any change.**

10 From Reference Check 1.0 to Reference Check 2.0

Reference Check 1.0 as shown above has many limitations and resides in the old fashion way of running your business. Today, as organizations are evolving towards digitization, they leverage more and more the latest way the Internet is used. Social networking is one of them. Reference checking is going to be transformed to the same extent and we at Checkster have observed it first hand. The only reaction we sometimes have is however that we need to have people interact and we need to rely on people not technology.

Paradoxically, Reference Check 2.0 does not rely less on people and more on technology — it relies more on people through technology.

Indeed Reference Check 1.0 gave you the assessment of 2.4 people on average while trying to reach 3 of them via phone. Today Reference Check 2.0 uses the medium that people use most (email communication) and reaps on average 5.5 references. It is relying more on people and less on formalities. It is not unusual to have witnessed individuals inviting 15 to 20 references. This is the normal extension of the increasingly connected way of life we live in and the social interactions that happen online.

We buy books, cars or vacations online, and to be even more personal according to some studies, 20 percent of Americans find love online.

But understand us well: we do not say that relying only on a Reference Check 2.0 to select a new employee is enough. Especially for people sharing offices and workspace (for company culture and fit), it is highly recommended to combine it with structured interviews.

What we are saying is that more and more people have the full updated contact information of their colleagues online. This makes the online interaction so easy and so normal that the request for feedback online is not only the most efficient but is expected.

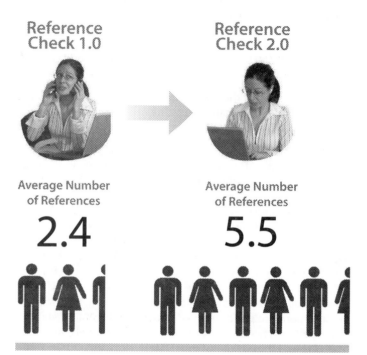

Fig 11. From Reference Check 1.0 to Reference Check 2.0

The added benefit for the employer is the fast turnaround (cut in half) and the efficiency of running it.

To summarize: Reference Check 2.0 is a normal evolution of our digital life. Digital social networks act as a recorder of our natural diverse social interactions, and consequently becomes a core enabler of gathering collective intelligence. When associated with the benefits of real time and true confidentiality, you have all the components of an accurate way to rely on the wisdom of the crowd.

One-sentence summary: **Reference Check 2.0 is becoming a central piece for work reputation.**

11 New possibilities with Reference Check 2.0

11. 1 Each job interview becomes a performance review

Across you can see the results from a survey we did on 154 reference checking practitioners. The question here was when are reference checks performed in the recruiting process?

As you can see, most organizations (84 percent) are performing reference checks after the selection has already been made. Unfortunately, this is only good to avoid a bad hire and not to insure a quality one. The reference check, when bundled with background checking, is mainly done to make sure the individual in question does not have criminal records, a drug history, or similar issues. If you want to leverage collective intelligence in order to screen the best people, you need to give the recruiter and the hiring manager the data before they make a decision. And typically the decision is not made when you still have a couple of finalists in the running. Today only 15 percent of organizations are performing reference checks on finalists. This is the best practice if you want to leverage reference checking to its full and impactful potential. More extreme and very rare (less than 1 percent) are performing reference checks on every individual coming in. This is obviously a very powerful way to screen individuals early and accurately, however, it can turn away some candidates.

Armed with a Reference Check 2.0, each job interview becomes more like a performance review, as you gain insight into the detailed review of colleagues on their achievement, strengths and areas in need of improvement.

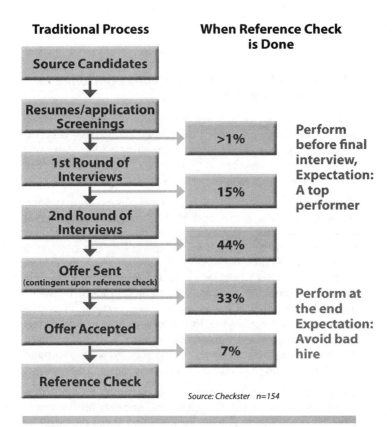

Fig 12. When Reference Check 1.0 is performed

To summarize: The Reference Check 2.0 gives you the potential to transform each job interview into a performance review-like discussion. To make it happen, you need to make sure it happens at a stage where you can still act on the intelligence that you receive. It should therefore be performed before you select one single candidate. Do it on all the final candidates.

One-sentence summary: **Reference Check 2.0 transforms each job interview into a performance review when done on several finalists.**

11. 2 Each Reference Check 2.0 is an opportunity for candid feedback

Today, among the companies that perform reference checks, one third of them are inconsistent. Two thirds (66.9 percent) perform it on at least 75 percent of their new hires. Very few perform it when they promote internally. Time pressure, cost, and speed are the traditional reasons.

By leveraging collective intelligence for recruiting or promotion purposes as the most cost-efficient way to gain great understanding and certainty about the quality of an individual, there are no more excuses for companies to not perform a reference check. Yet some organizations will not want to perform it on roles that are not seen as pivotal. Pivotal employees are defined as critical value creators for an organization. However, it is often difficult in many organizations to distinguish pivotal from non-pivotal employees. The typical example of the cleaners in the Disney parks as being pivotal employees shed some light on how we can fool ourselves. Consequently, we recommend knowing the limited cost to do it for all.

But more importantly, we see the opportunity to perform a Reference Check 2.0 for all finalists and not only for the single selected candidate as a good business and social practice. By giving a feedback 2.0 to the individual, it is also a good social practice. Indeed, we have often seen individuals receive such feedback, good or not, for the first time in their lives. As described by Jack Welch, the lack of candid feedback is the biggest dirty little secret of business. Feedback is the only way we truly learn and adapt, and providing this venue for each finalist when well positioned will do more for your employment brand than any advertising you may run. It simply shows that you care about your employees, and want to give them something useful to help them grow.

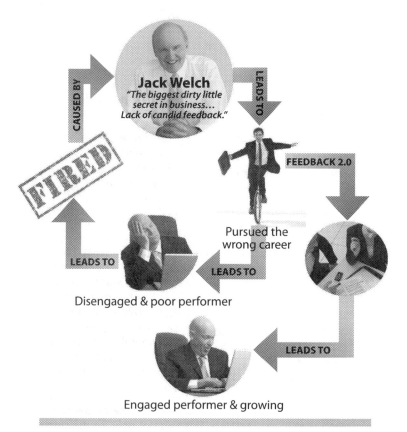

Fig 13. Virtuous cycle of candid feedback

To summarize: Reference Check 2.0 should be performed on all job changes, internal or external, pivotal or not. It is not only the most cost efficient way to gain the most accurate details about the individual, but it is also a social act. When well performed, it provides feedback to the candidates to help them grow and improve. That will do more for your employment brand than any ad you may run.

One-sentence summary: **Sharing the feedback from the Reference Check 2.0 with the candidate will help them grow and brand you well.**

11. 3 Each Reference Check 2.0 gathers passive candidates:

In the traditional process of gathering pre-hire references, the contacts you will typically make are then lost. They may reside in the candidate folder and not be reactivated any more. Few companies or agencies use them. Search firms on the other hand work carefully on their database and each reference is a potential future candidate or even customer.

This typically work-intensive activity performed on the three to five references that are collected per candidate often reap good results. This is especially true when all the contacts are put in a searchable database. Indeed, for instance, if you now search for a lawyer with expertise in a typical industry, you can type the keywords related to the title associated with the company names where they may have worked. You can then find highly targeted individuals who are most likely passive candidates from your reference list.

The passive candidate database that Reference Check 2.0 relies on is based on the same principle, but is just completely automated. Since all the references are automatically put in a database, it is now possible to keyword search the references' employers, title, area code, and of course name or even the name of the person they have been referred by. That provides you with a nice network that automatically builds itself with no effort.

The power of such databases becomes even more interesting as the Reference Check 2.0 relies on social networks to boost the number of references typically provided.

Indeed, it is not unusual to see a candidate refer 15 to 20 references with on average about nine references submitted.

So if you are hiring 1,000 people a year, you are likely to have close to 10,000 passive candidates automatically added to your pool for active search.

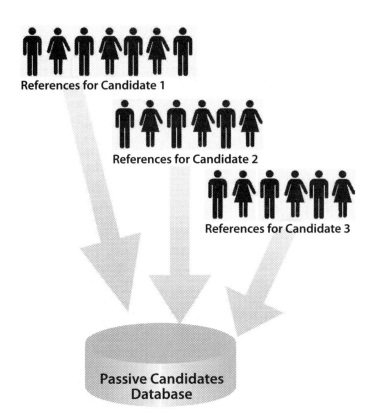

Fig 14. Reference Check 2.0 automated passive candidates gathering

To summarize: Reference Check 2.0 capitalizes on the increased number of references collected by storing them in a searchable database. You are then transforming a one off relationship into a connection that can be leveraged when you are looking for such talent in the future.

One-sentence summary: **References given for a Reference Check 2.0 are stored and searchable.**

Appendices

1 Reference Check Questionnaire Form

Position Applied For:	Candidate Name:
Requisition #:	Telephone Number:

❶ Checklist before calling:

☐ Candidate signed a written consent form
☐ Candidate signed a release of liabilities form
☐ I am aware of illegal follow up questions (if not see end of questionnaire)
☐ Did you add job specific attributes to question 8?

❷ Details of reference:

Date:

Reference Name:

Reference Telephone Number:

Current Employer:

Current Position:

Position when working with candidate:

IF REFERENCE ANSWERS, START BELOW:

[Candidate Name] gave me your name as a reference.

S/he is being considered for employment at our organization and I wanted to ask you a couple of questions.

[Candidate] has signed a consent and a release form that authorizes the release of information related to his/her work performance.

Is it ok to ask you a couple of questions now? It shouldn't take more than 10 minutes.

IF OK, PROCEED TO Q1

IF NOT A GOOD TIME, ASK: when would be a suitable time?

IF COMPANY POLICY PROHIBITS THE REFERENCE FROM GIVING ANY INFORMATION, SAY:

Can you at least respond to the purely factual data about the employee?

IF YES, GO TO Q1

IF NO, CLOSE.

1. What is/was your main connection to [Candidate Name]? You are/were a:
   - ☐ Peer
   - ☐ Supervisor
   - ☐ Subordinate
   - ☐ Friend   ⇢ **IF SELECTED, ASSESS IF YOU SHOULD CONTINUE**
   - ☐ Professor
   - ☐ Client
   - ☐ Other   ⇢ **IF SELECTED, ASSESS IF YOU SHOULD CONTINUE**

2. How current is your relationship with [Candidate Name]?
   - ☐ Currently interact or work together
   - ☐ Worked or interacted in the last 2 years
   - ☐ Worked or interacted 2-5 years ago
     ⇢ **IF SELECTED, ASSESS IF YOU SHOULD CONTINUE**
   - ☐ Worked or interacted 5+ years ago
     ⇢ **IF SELECTED, ASSESS IF YOU SHOULD CONTINUE**

3. How long did you work/interact together?
   - ☐ Less than 6 months
     ⇢ **IF SELECTED, ASSESS IF YOU SHOULD CONTINUE**
   - ☐ Between 6 and 18 months
     ⇢ **IF SELECTED, ASSESS IF YOU SHOULD CONTINUE**
   - ☐ Between 18 months and 3 years
   - ☐ More than 3 years

4. Did you work:
   ☐ in direct contact
   ☐ sometimes on same projects
   ☐ rarely on same projects
      ⇢ **IF SELECTED, ASSESS IF YOU SHOULD CONTINUE**
   ☐ Other   ⇢ **IF SELECTED, ASSESS IF YOU SHOULD CONTINUE**

5. What would you say are/were [Candidate Name]'s top 3 key strengths?

6. What would you say is/was [Candidate Name]'s most significant accomplishment with your organization?

7. What would you say are/were [Candidate Name]'s top 3 areas that need improvement to increase professional performance?

6. If you had the opportunity, would you hire or recommend hiring [Candidate Name] again?

From 1 to 7 with 1=Not at all likely, 7=Very likely

CIRCLE: 1   2   3   4   5   6   7

IF 4 or BELOW ASK: Why such a rating?

7. How would you rate the overall quality of [Candidate Name]'s job performance?

From 1 to 7 with 1=Not good quality, 7=Very good quality

CIRCLE: 1   2   3   4   5   6   7

IF 4 or BELOW ASK: Why such a rating?

8. Do you respect [Candidate Name] for the following:

From 1 to 7 with1 = no respect, 4 = average, 7 = total respect

	CIRCLE THE RESPONSE: NO RESPECT TOTAL RESPECT						
Mastery of industry and product knowledge	1	2	3	4	5	6	7
Exhibiting relevant behaviors for job success	1	2	3	4	5	6	7
Work related skills	1	2	3	4	5	6	7
Ability to display energy in all tasks	1	2	3	4	5	6	7
Ability to make decisions in a timely manner	1	2	3	4	5	6	7
Ability to execute and create results	1	2	3	4	5	6	7
Delivers work on time	1	2	3	4	5	6	7
Consistently provides quality results	1	2	3	4	5	6	7
Effectively deals with complex situations	1	2	3	4	5	6	7
Is widely trusted and seen as truthful	1	2	3	4	5	6	7
Effectively handles pressure and stress	1	2	3	4	5	6	7
Is seen as a team player	1	2	3	4	5	6	7
Understands company's strategic vision	1	2	3	4	5	6	7
Keeps promises, is dependable	1	2	3	4	5	6	7
:	1	2	3	4	5	6	7
:	1	2	3	4	5	6	7
:	1	2	3	4	5	6	7

IF 4 or BELOW ASK: Why such a rating?

2 Best Reference Check Questions Explanations

The following sections explain the type of questions that are used in the reference check form.

2.1 Qualifying questions

The most important element in a reference check is to make sure the reference is a qualified individual. Too often we rush into our questionnaire and realize that we have wasted time speaking to someone who has not worked with the candidate in 10 years or more. At Checkster, we categorize a qualified individual according to four factors:

> *Too often we rush into our questionnaire and realize that we have wasted time speaking to a colleague that last worked with the candidate 10 years ago!*

- Freshness of the relationship (how recently did you work together?)
- Length of the relationship (how long did you work together?)
- Closeness of the interaction (how close did you work together?)
- Nature of the relationship (are you a peer, subordinate, friend, etc.?)

1. **Freshness of the relationship:** Ideally, you want references that are still working with the candidate, and certainly not references that are more than 18 months old. If the candidate has been employed for more than 18 months and is still employed there, ask for references that used to work with him/her. If those are not enough, ask them to perform a Checkster 360 Checkup at the same time of the Reference Checkup. They'll have the option as part of your email invitation to perform a 360 Checkup, and won't necessarily have to disclose information contained in the concurrent Reference Checkup to their colleagues.

2. **Length of the relationship:** What is the value of having a reference that has only worked two hours with the individual? Not much better than your exposure to the candidate

during the interview. This qualification avoids wasting time questioning those who can provide little to no information about a candidate's performance. Make sure people have worked at least 18 months together.

3. **The closeness of the interaction:** We often confuse working in the same company with working together. Sharing lunch together or large company meetings is not enough to know the intrinsic value of an individual. Make sure to question people who have worked on the same projects with your candidate.

4. **Nature of the relationship:** It is less valuable to receive feedback from friends and family than it is from peers, subordinates, or bosses. Each has its value, as peers offer more insight into one's true performance, whereas bosses can explain how to manage the individual, and subordinates can uncover how good a leader the individual is.

2.2 Open-ended questions

The difficulty in doing reference checks often lies in the use of leading questions such as, "Do you think the candidate's strength is closing sales?" The formulation of the question itself disrupts what we are looking for. In order to truly know what distinguishes an individual from any other is to start with open-ended questions. Asking general questions about one's strengths, accomplishments, and areas in need of improvement is a good start. Yet, those questions, if not prompted by any specific context will push people to think about the individual in general terms. If specific accomplishments and strengths are revealed at this stage, then you are likely looking at a good candidate.

2.3 Net Promoter question

Bain and Company noticed[5] that the most effective way to predict future growth and profit for a business is by asking one question: "Would you recommend this product to a friend?"

---

[5] The Ultimate Question: Driving Good Profits and True Growth by Fred Reichheld, Harvard Business School Press, 2006

What we recommend here at Checkster is to apply this same principle to people. This has in fact been in action in leading companies such as Hewlett Packard, with whom we consulted in the past. The variance of this question is: "Would you re-hire this individual again?" Top performers will always be recommended, and others will require qualification. This simple question is the equivalent of the net promoter question for individuals, and as simple as it seems, the answer will provide you with a clear indication of one's overall estimation of the candidate.

Another variant of this, which assesses the readiness of being promoted, is also very important, especially when you are hiring someone as a step up in their career. In other words, a simple question such as, "Do you think he/she is ready to be promoted?" will give you an indication of the candidate's possible shortcomings.

2.4 Attitude Questions

There is a saying in recruiting: "You hire for skills and fire for attitude." Consequently, it is very important to make sure you have a grasp of the attitude traits of the candidate — from their energy level to their integrity. A full list of traits can be found on the recommended questionnaire in the walk through section.

Note that it is good for you to know among specific characteristics, which are crucial ones versus nice-to-have ones for a specific job. For instance, for an individual contributor with limited interaction with other employees, it is not critical for him or her to be able to motivate others or be a top team player.

One important aspect here is to try to reduce the pollution in the rating when one is speaking from an emotional view, which can be linked to any human relationship. Thus, the best way to ask these questions is to consequently ask if the references "respect" the individual for his or her level of energy, dependability, or integrity. In short, you may not like the individual, but can still admit that his or her level of dependability is exceptional.

2.5 Specific knowledge and skills questions

For each job there are a couple of specific must-haves. They can often be learned, but unless you hire young graduates, you expect experienced people to have a grasp of those specifics. For instance, at Checkster we allow recruiters or hiring managers to include specific questions at the end of the online questionnaire.

One of our customers in the financial industry required deep analytical skills and SPSS knowledge. They specifically asked the candidate's colleagues questions regarding these skills. Note that they can be used as a complement to pure packaged skill tests available on various tools (i.e. Excel fluency, etc.). Such qualities and characteristics are important to know prior to the interview or any reference check process. In other words, it is very important that you make your best effort to identify the specific knowledge and skills that are required for you to hire a top performer.

You can't hire a top performer if you have not defined what one is!

3 Reference Check 2.0 Versus Reference Check 1.0

Both methods have different advantages and disadvantages and are in no way exclusive.

In the new Reference Check 2.0 process, we recommend to always start by leveraging an online method and to follow up optionally with a selective phone process for questionable candidates or to qualify further aspects of the applicant.

Many people that are good at running reference checks over the phone are often reluctant to do so online. It is a little bit like it was during the beginning of online retail, when some people still preferred to have the actual store experience.

But similar to retail, some hiring situations will make it very appropriate to be 100 percent online, whereas others will contain a good mixture of first round online reference checks more like an assessment followed by telephone surveys. A minority of those situations will be exclusively over the phone. The arguments in favor of each technique are summarized below.

	Reference Check 2.0	**Reference Check 1.0**
Advantages	Low workload Reach more references More accurate results Responses are more truthful Automatic aggregation of references as potential candidates Legally safe	Ability to have follow up questions Impression to be able to judge intangibles* (tone of voice, etc.)
Disadvantages	No on-the-spot follow up questions Not possible for people with no online access	Time consuming Not consistent Hard to take notes and document well Legally risky

*Note that we list this one as it is often mentioned as an advantage, even though we think that not knowing the reference's character (i.e. If the individual is cynical or upbeat) makes us question the absolute validity of this statement.

4 Reference Check 2.0 process in image

SCREEN EXAMPLE	STEP	MANAGER TIME REQUIRED

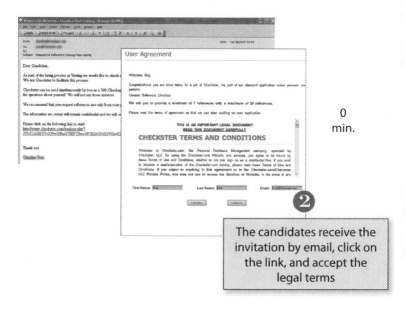

① Invite candidate by email to perform a reference checkup

(Ideally for all 3 to 5 final candidates)

1-2 min.

0 min.

② The candidates receive the invitation by email, click on the link, and accept the legal terms

SCREEN EXAMPLE	STEP	MANAGER TIME REQUIRED

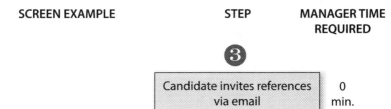

Candidate invites references via email	0 min.

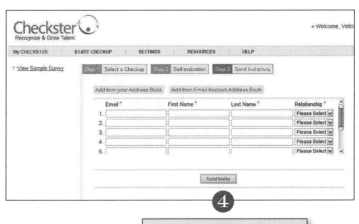

References respond to an online tailored questionnaire	0 min.

The standard reference questionnaire has 15 questions.

Reference Check 2.0 report

SCREEN EXAMPLE	STEP	MANAGER TIME REQUIRED

	You review the report that is automatically generated	2-5 min.

Report Sections Description:

1. Top Line Summary:

Checkster methodology **focuses on performance** rather than skills

Easy to read top line results that focus on the individual performance. 100% best, 0% worst.

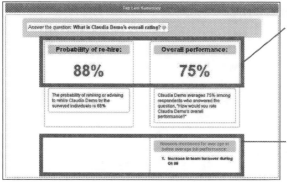

If any reference rates the individual average or below s/he will be prompted to specify.

Methodology details: Bain and Company noticed[6] that the most effective way to predict future growth and profit for a business is by asking one question: "Would you recommend this product to a friend?" What we recommend at Checkster is to apply this same principle to people. This has in fact been in action in leading companies such as Hewlett Packard, with whom we consulted in the past. The variance of this question is: "Would you re-hire this individual again?" Top performers will always be recommended, and others will require qualification. This simple question is the equivalent of the net promoter question for individuals, and as simple as it seems, the answer will provide you with a clear indication of one's overall estimation of the candidate.

---

[6] The Ultimate Question: Driving Good Profits and True Growth by Fred Reichheld, Harvard Business School Press, 2006

2. Open Ended Questions:

Checkster offers **non leading questions to truly uncover key strengths.**

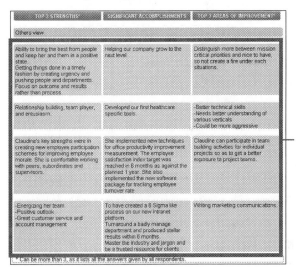

Checkster methodology starts with open-ended questions on strengths, accomplishments and areas in need of improvements. Those guarantee non leading answers and focus on more than mere endorsements.

Methodology details: The difficulty in doing reference checks often lies in the use of leading questions such as, "Do you think the candidate's strength is in closing sales?" The formulation of the question itself disrupts what we are looking for. In order to truly know what distinguishes an individual from any other is to start with open-ended questions. Asking general questions about one's strengths, accomplishments, and areas in need of improvement is a good start. Yet, those questions, if not prompted by any specific context will push people to think about the individual in general terms. If specific accomplishments and strengths are revealed at this stage, then you are likely looking at a good candidate.

3. 15 Tailorable Attribute Questions:

Checkster's 15 attribute questions enable **specific tailorable rating** on important factors.

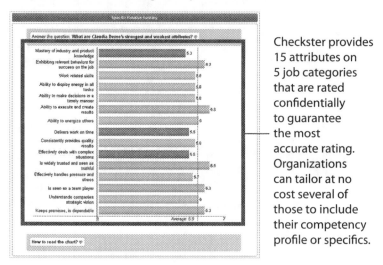

Checkster provides 15 attributes on 5 job categories that are rated confidentially to guarantee the most accurate rating. Organizations can tailor at no cost several of those to include their competency profile or specifics.

Methodology details: There is a saying in recruiting: "You hire for skills and fire for attitude." Consequently, it is very important to make sure you have a grasp of the attitude traits of the candidate — from their energy level to their integrity. A list of traits and specific behaviors by job categories can be found on the standard Checkster questionnaire. One important aspect here is to try to reduce the pollution in the rating when one is speaking from an emotional view, which can be linked to any human relationship. Thus, the best way to ask these questions is to consequently ask if the references "respect" the individual for his or her level of energy, dependability, or integrity. In short, you may not like the individual, but can still admit that his or her level of dependability is exceptional. Note that you can tailor many of those yourself at no additional cost.

4. Self-service Optional Questions:

Selected users can add tailored questions in real time at no cost.

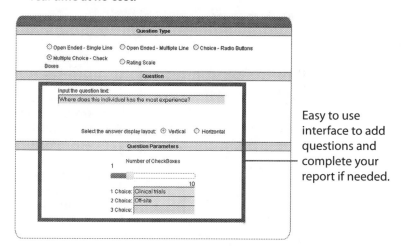

Easy to use interface to add questions and complete your report if needed.

Methodology details: For each job there are a couple of specific must-haves. They can often be learned, but unless you hire young graduates, you expect experienced people to have a grasp of those specifics. For instance, at Checkster we allow recruiters or hiring managers to include specific questions at the end of the online questionnaire. One of our customers in the financial industry required deep analytical skills and SPSS knowledge. They specifically asked the candidate's colleagues questions regarding these skills. Note that they can be used as a complement to pure packaged skill tests available on various tools (i.e. Excel fluency, etc.). Such qualities and characteristics are important to know prior to the interview or any reference check process. In other words, it is very important that you make your best effort to identify the specific knowledge and skills that are required for you to hire a top performer.

5. Qualification of References:

Easy to read **4 dimensional qualifications of references.**

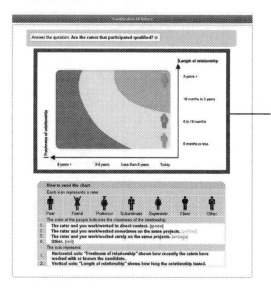

Green and yellow people of the right shapes insure maximum qualification of the raters.

We are not only asking for titles and when they interacted, but also how close they interacted and for how long.

Methodology details: The most important element in a reference check is to make sure the reference is a qualified individual. Too often we rush into our questionnaire and realize that we have wasted time speaking to someone who has not worked with the candidate in 10 years or more. At Checkster, we categorize a qualified individual according to four factors:

- Freshness of the relationship (how recently did you work together?)
- Length of the relationship (how long did you work together?)
- Closeness of the interaction (how close did you work together?)
- Nature of the relationship (are you a peer, subordinate, friend, etc.?)

1. **Freshness of the relationship:** Ideally, you want references that are still working with the candidate, and certainly not references that are more than 18 months old. If the candidate has been employed for more than 18 months and is still employed there, ask for references

that used to work with him/her. If those are not enough, ask them to perform a Checkster 360 Checkup at the same time of the Reference Checkup. They'll have the option as part of your email invitation to perform a 360 Checkup, and won't necessarily have to disclose information contained in the concurrent Reference Checkup to their colleagues.

2. **Length of the relationship:** What is the value of having a reference that has only worked two hours with the individual? Not much better than your exposure to the candidate during the interview. This qualification avoids wasting time questioning those who can provide little to no information about a candidate's performance. Make sure people have worked at least 18 months together.

3. **The closeness of the interaction:** We often confuse working in the same company with working together. Sharing lunch together or large company meetings is not enough to know the intrinsic value of an individual. Make sure to question people who have worked on the same projects with your candidate.

4. **Nature of the relationship:** It is less valuable to receive feedback from friends and family than it is from peers, subordinates, or bosses. Each has its value, as peers offer more insight into one's true performance, whereas bosses can explain how to manage the individual, and subordinates can uncover how good a leader the individual is.

6. Certification of the References:

Tracking of email domains, IP and cookies **prevent fraud.**

Checkster will flag you when the source of references may be at risk.

Methodology details: Although rare, some candidates may try to game the online tool. For that reason, Checkster monitors all the IP, the cookies and the email domains to make sure to flag potential fraud. Individuals that try to invite fake email addresses or respond on behalf of their colleagues will be flagged.

7. Filtering of the References:

Ability to **filter dynamically** the results according to role.

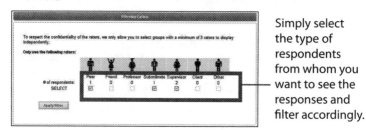

Simply select the type of respondents from whom you want to see the responses and filter accordingly.

Methodology details: Checkster enables you to see the results by role type assuming that you have the required minimum raters per role. This enables you to see, for instance in this example, what peers are thinking versus supervisors. This is a very powerful way to cut the data in more detail.

8. List of References with Contact Details:

List of references for additional follow up and automatic inclusion in database of passive candidates.

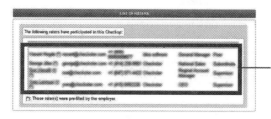

All references are listed with their details and contact information as well as stored for potential follow up or future passive candidate search.

9. Complimentary Employment Verification:

Checkster provides a **complimentary optional employment verification.**

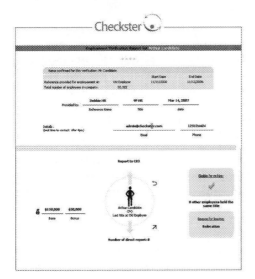

Gives the details of the person giving the employment verification as well as the organization's details.

Provides key traditional factual data such as reporting structure, eligibility for rehire, salary and reason for leaving.

Methodology details: Checkster enables all users of its application to request employment verifications using the same process as the reference check. Sent to a past manager or HR representative by the candidate, this Checkup only focuses on factual data that HR organizations are required legally to provide to prospective employers. The Employment Verification report includes: your candidate's date of employment; reporting structure; compensation; eligibility for re-hire; and reason for leaving, as well as the candidate's name and title.

6 Reference Check 2.0 ROI

The use of Reference Check 2.0 has two clear benefits:

1. Increased quality outcome (better reference checks and consequently better hires).

2. A more efficient process.

Even though the quality of hires has a strong financial impact on an organization, they are harder to prove and consequently less often relied upon by financial executives. Operational executives on the other hand, clearly understand the huge benefit organizations gain by employing great employees, as well as the detriment poor hires cause by dragging down performance. It is estimated in the industry that a mis-hire costs on average, one time the yearly salary of that individual.

Imagine what a 5 percent increase in productivity would do for your company's financial outlook if new hires were just 5 percent better. These measurements are at the core of true strategic talent management. Return On Investment (ROI) exercises are designed for cost-driven mindsets, so we will focus the benefits on the directly observable savings. We do however encourage you to monitor the top line benefits you will gain by utilizing such processes, for in them is where the huge ROI will appear.

How is Reference Check 2.0 more efficient?

The process described in this document offloads the core of the work to the automation tool and the candidate. The core benefits are then on the time saved to perform the traditional reference check.

The tasks involved in a traditional reference check are:

1. Request a list of references from the candidate

2. Send the candidate a consent form

3. Receive signed consent form from candidate

4. Receive a list of references

5. Call (leave message) or email the references to set an appointment to discuss the candidate

6. Call time is confirmed

7. Call takes place

8. Consolidate notes taken during each call to create a presentable report

9. Repeat steps 5-8 for each reference

A traditional reference check process attempts to contact 3 references, but only successfully reaches 2.4 on average. The time taken by recruiters or hiring managers to perform tasks described above is 76 minutes.

On the other hand, when you use a Reference Check 2.0, the time it takes to initiate the Reference Checkup is less than two minutes. The time required to read the report often takes less than five minutes. We will estimate conservatively that a Reference Checkup process requires 7 minutes of a recruiter or hiring manager's time. Again, we will not make the case for the increased consistency, reliability and amount of references received (5.5 on average). We are strictly making the case for the cost savings made on the pure activities.

For each hire you are saving over an hour of time for the person who performs the process, and by accounting for the cost of the service delivering the Reference Check 2.0, you will often reach a 50% ROI.

> **Summary:** Reference Check 2.0 benefits from a 50%+ ROI just on the pure process of saving time. If you take into account the improvement on quality gained by such an approach, your ROI is a factor of 10 to 100 more.

7 How to start using a Reference Check 2.0 process

If you find that the recommendations given in this book can help you, please start using them. They are also incorporated in the Checkster tool.

To watch an audio visual intro to Checkster, visit:
http://www.checkster.com/web/pre-hire.php

To start, follow this link:
http://www.checkster.com/web/pre-start.php

About the author:

Yves Lermusi (aka Lermusiaux) is CEO & founder of **Checkster**.

Checkster is a Career and Talent Checkup tool.

Mr. Lermusi founded Checkster after seven years at Taleo (TLEO) as President of Taleo Research. Prior to Taleo, Mr. Lermusi founded iLogos (acquired by Taleo) and held several positions in research and consulting organizations in Europe.

Mr. Lermusi is a well known public speaker and a Career and Talent industry commentator. He is often quoted in the leading business media worldwide, including Fortune, The Wall Street Journal, Financial Times, Business Week, and Time Magazine. His articles and commentary are published regularly in online publications and business magazines. Mr. Lermusi was named one of the "100 Most Influential People in the Recruiting Industry" and his blog has been recognized as the best third party blog.

Mr. Lermusi earned a degree in Physics and Philosophy, and has a diploma in Economics from the University of Brussels and from the University of London.

Mr. Lermusi currently lives in Mill Valley, California with his wife and three children.

About Checkster:

Checkster stands for giving individuals and organizations tools that will help them recognize and grow their talent. Checkster aims to improve the world's productivity and harmony by increasing job fit and work achievement, as well as personal career satisfaction and fulfillment.

Checkster provides Personal Feedback tools that are revolutionizing traditional 360 degree feedback methodologies and employer reference checks. Individuals now have unprecedented access to tools that help them grow and develop within their career. Employers can leverage Checkster to hire, retain, and grow the right talent.

Founded in 2006 by Yves Lermusi (aka Lermusiaux), a talent management industry veteran, Checkster leverages the latest technology and research in expert performance and neuroscience.

To learn more about what Checkster can do for your organization, visit http://www.checkster.com